MARGARET AND JOHN TRAVERS MOORE

PEPITO'S SPEECH

AT THE UNITED NATIONS

illustrated and designed by

DENISE & FERNANDO

United Nations

A UNITED NATIONS publication

Printed in New York

UNITED NATIONS
New York, N.Y. 10017
USA   00595

PEPITO'S SPEECH

AT THE UNITED NATIONS
and the PEPITO BOOKS

Pepito's Speech at the United Nations is the first book of fiction and first children's book published by the United Nations. It was issued as a commemorative of the UN's 40th Anniversary.

Translated into many languages, it has been adopted for classroom use in various countries, and is approved by the National Education Association.

Pepito's Speech was selected for the Golden Balloon Award by the child delegates at the United Nations from 150 nations on World Children's Day. The award is for "an outstanding contribution to children".

Pepito's Speech was so popular that *Pepito's Journey* (the second book) reached an established group of Pepito's fans around the world, and was soon followed by *Pepito's World*. The three books have a universal theme, the quest for peace.

In *Pepito's Speech*, a little boy visits the United Nations and brings to the world, kindness, a single smile and a dream of peace understood by all people of the world.

Pepito with his smile and dream, goes to Latin America in *Pepito's Journey*; he calls attention to the plight of the homeless in all lands.

In *Pepito's World*, he learns the value of sharing with friends at home and abroad. That changes his life and the life of a crippled boy. As a result the world comes to him in a children's year of international friendship.

The United States Mission to the United Nations has suggested that *Pepito's World* be incorporated in the World Decade of Cultural Development 1988-1997 as designated by the General Assembly of the United Nations "since the book establishes a global communication among young people". Thus, it has been placed with the Secretariat of the United Nations Educational, Scientific and Cultural Organization whose Headquarters are in Paris.

Of *Pepito's World*, Vernon A. Walters, former United States Ambassador to the United Nations, expressed appreciation for its "sincere dedication to promoting peace and an outlook of friendship among the youth of the world."

The Authors

MARGARET and JOHN TRAVERS MOORE sometimes col-
laborated on their children's books and at other times they worked
separately. This book is dedicated to a friend of the authors who
served his neighbours and the cause of peace in other lands.

John Travers Moore, considered one of America's leading children's poets, and his author-wife Margaret combined their talents to
offer this sincere-hearted story to boys and girls of all countries.

The Illustrators

Pepito's Speech at the United Nations, a timeless message first
published as a trade book in 1971, was re-published by the United
Nations in 1985. Two preceding illustrations of Pepito in *Pepito's
Speech* have been made by illustrators. This one, by DENISE
FRAIFELD and FERNANDO AZEVEDO, complements their illustrations in *Pepito's Journey* and *Pepito's World* to complete and make
uniform the Pepito Books.

DENISE and FERNANDO are very well known in Brazil and
throughout Latin America for their creative illustrations for books
designed for children.

During the recent Bratislava International Biennial in Czecho-
slovakia, the artists were awarded a "Golden Plaquette" for one of
their works selected from among 2,300 illustrations from 50 countries
by a jury composed of representatives of 20 countries.

Denise was born in 1958 and Fernando in 1954 in Rio de Ja-
neiro, Brazil, where they still reside.

UNITED NATIONS

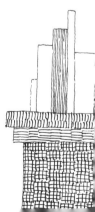

Pepito liked to smile and he liked to listen. He was not very big but his big sunny smile made everyone smile back at him. And everybody knew that but Pepito. Pepito knew only that he liked to smile.

Pepito was a peacemaker. If his classmates in school quarreled, they would stop when Pepito joined them. If the boys in his neighborhood started to fight, Pepito would smile and they would stop fighting.

Pepito learned much by listening and smiling. He heard people speak of the United Nations. They said it was a place where nations of the world could meet to discuss their problems and work for world peace. Being a peacemaker, Pepito was very interested.

He heard more about the United Nations in

school and on television. There seemed to be much disagreement among its members. "Why must nations quarrel?" Pepito wondered. "Why can't they learn to get along with one another?" He thought about this for a long time. And the more he thought, the more positive he became that something should be done to help the United Nations bring peace to the world.

One evening at the dinner table Pepito made a decision. On the plate before him was a generous helping of Spanish rice. There were also Danish rolls, Swiss cheese, and a crisp lettuce salad with French dressing. Pepito knew what the dessert would be—American apple pie.

"The United Nations should be like this dinner," thought Pepito. "All parts go well together."

But before he took one bite, he sat up straight and announced, "I am going to make a speech!"

"Hear, hear!" said Pepito's father. He laid down his knife and fork to listen.

"I am going to make a speech to the United

Nations," Pepito continued.

"Oh," said his father, picking up his knife and fork again. "What country will you represent?"

"All countries," said Pepito.

"And what will your speech be about?" asked his father.

"The United Nations and peace."

"That's a big subject," said Pepito's father.

Pepito knew that his father was right, but he was determined to help the United Nations. He would start immediately to prepare his speech.

After dinner Pepito went out to sit on the fire escape of his apartment building. It was a wonderful place to think. It had a pleasant view and was quiet at this hour except for the noise of traffic far below.

Pepito looked to his left. There in the distance stood the United Nations building, tall and magnificent. Its many windows gleamed in the slanting rays of the lowering sun.

Pepito looked to his right. He could not see it, but he knew the Statue of Liberty stood there

holding up her torch to welcome people to America's shores.

In the middle, between the Statue of Liberty and the United Nations building, Mrs. O'Leary's laundry hung in neat rows, and so Pepito could not see much in that direction.

But there was a feeling of bigness all about him. Pepito breathed deeply of the early evening air and listened to the rumbling of automobiles below. "It is a fine world," he said. "It is made for big things. The United Nations should be proud to represent and protect it."

Every evening Pepito went out on the fire escape to work on his speech. Each night he looked to the right toward the Statue of Liberty and to the left at the United Nations building. He wondered what was in the middle beyond Mrs. O'Leary's washing, or Mrs. Callahan's, or Mrs. Aufheiser's, or that of the Widow Pulaski, who took in other people's washing and completely filled the lines.

Night after night Pepito worked on his speech, sometimes frowning as a sudden wind blew a ruddy lock of hair across his forehead, sometimes sitting quietly, clear eyes staring at the sky, searching for a word that would not come. And always, as the right word finally came, a wide smile would appear on his round, freckled face. Pepito did not write his speech. He memorized it, every word in order, because it was exactly what he thought and felt in his heart.

As days went by, Pepito continued to listen and learn. He found new things to add to his United Nations speech. Even when there was an argument between Mr. Graccioso, who owned the fruit store, and Mr. Roberts, who owned the candy shop, Pepito found an idea in it.

Mr. Roberts and Mr. Graccioso argued about war so heatedly that they themselves seemed ready to fight. But when they glanced down they saw Pepito smiling at them. They smiled back and then noticed that it was a fine morning. Soon Mr. Graccioso was busy selling juicy North American pears and large yellow South American bananas to a Greek gentleman and his Armenian wife. And at the same time next door Mr. Roberts was talking with his customers in three different languages.

"It is the spirit of the United Nations,"

thought Pepito. "Nations, like people, must learn to live together. I shall put that in my speech."

Pepito gathered more and more information for his speech. Each time that he added some-thing new to it, he smiled, but his smile was biggest when the speech was completed.

"I'm ready," he said, looking first toward the Statue of Liberty, then at the United Nations building, then at Mrs. Pulaski's washing on the line in front of him. The shirts and slacks and dresses did not seem to be shirts or slacks or dresses at all, but people—many people.

"Delegates of the United Nations," began Pepito, starting his speech. He went through it from beginning to end. It was a fine speech—a speech that he believed would help solve the problems of the world.

Of course, there was no applause when he finished. The people in front of him once again became the shirts and slacks and dresses of Mrs. Pulaski's laundry.

"But someone must hear me practice my

speech before I give it to the United Nations," thought Pepito. "How else can I be sure it is right?"

He ran to ask his father. Then he stopped. No, his father was very busy working during the day, and in the evening he went to night school.

His mother? No, she was busy keeping house and cooking. Even in the evening she was busy planning for tomorrow.

Mr. Graccioso or Mr. Roberts?

Pepito hurried to Mr. Graccioso's fruit store and again found him arguing with Mr. Roberts. Pepito smiled up at them and said, "Do you want to hear my speech?"

Mr. Graccioso and Mr. Roberts looked down at Pepito. "What speech?" they asked.

"I am going to speak to the United Nations and tell them how they can stop the people of the world from fighting," said Pepito.

"Ha, ha, ha," laughed Mr. Roberts. "Pepito thinks he can stop people from fighting. What do you think of that, Mr. Graccioso?"

Mr. Graccioso shook his head.

"I have such a fine speech," insisted Pepito. "Don't you want to hear it?"

"I must take care of my customers," said Mr. Roberts, seeing a man enter his candy shop next door.

"And I have much work to do," said Mr. Graccioso. He picked up a red apple and polished it on his clean white apron.

Pepito was disappointed. He walked down the crowded city street. Women were busy shopping and talking with storekeepers. Newsboys were calling out headlines of the afternoon editions. Everywhere the hurrying throng was tending to the day's affairs.

Pepito entered a neighborhood park and sat down on a bench. He could hear the faint tune of a merry-go-round, the excited voices of children splashing water in the wading pool, and the shouts of other children at play. He watched idly as a sailor fed crumbs to pigeons. A mother pushed a baby carriage down the path in front of him, and an old couple strolled through patterns of sunlight made by a tall maple tree.

"There should be *someone* to listen to my speech," thought Pepito. But in his heart he knew that no one would listen. The world was too busy. In this great city of millions of people there was not one person who wanted to hear Pepito's speech.

An alley cat, skeleton-like, slunk by—a mere gray wisp of a cat. When Pepito saw it he called out, "You will listen to my speech!" But the cat, seeing no food, moved on.

"You, too!" said Pepito, discouraged. He cupped his chin in his hands and stared straight ahead. From all the stories he had read, he knew that now was the time for something to happen

—something which would help the hero. But nothing happened. Nothing at all.

Pepito went home but he was not smiling as much as usual. When he sat down at the dinner table he was very quiet.

"Pepito…" his mother began, noticing that something was wrong.

His father said, "This time it is I who have an announcement."

Pepito listened half-heartedly.

"You are so interested in the United Nations," said his father, "that your mother and I have decided to take you there."

Suddenly Pepito's eyes grew bright. His big smile was back. "You—will take me?"

"Tomorrow," promised his father. His mother smiled down at Pepito because he was smiling so broadly.

"I can make my speech!" said Pepito.

"Do you have such a speech?" asked his father.

"Yes," Pepito said. "I wanted to practice it but no one would listen. That doesn't matter now. I shall give my speech at the United Nations. It is a good speech—an excellent speech! I know they will like it!"

"Pepito," his mother said, "you are only a little boy. Little boys do not give speeches at the United Nations."

"It is a very fine speech," insisted Pepito. "It will bring peace to the world."

Pepito's father and mother shook their heads doubtfully. A little boy give a speech at the United Nations? It was impossible!

"We shall have to convince Pepito," his father said to his mother that evening. "Children don't give speeches at the United Nations."

"I hope he won't be too disappointed," his mother worried.

Pepito himself was not worrying at all. He was thinking about how he would go to the United Nations and give the speech he had so carefully thought out and memorized. He would tell people from all over the world how to live peacefully together.

The next morning Pepito and his mother and father awoke very early. "We'll make a day of it," his father said. "We'll start early and have lunch at the United Nations. We can take a guided tour and you will be able to see everything."

As they started on their way, they passed Mr. Graccioso standing in front of his fruit store. "What nice pears you have!" said Pepito's mother.

Mr. Graccioso looked pleased.

Mr. Roberts was in his candy shop next door. "How's business?" asked Pepito's father.

"Fine," Mr. Roberts replied.

"That's good," smiled Pepito's father.

While they waited at the corner for a bus, Mrs. Pulaski appeared in the doorway of her apartment building and shook out her dust mop. "Where are you going?" she called to them.

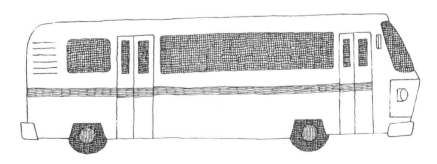

"To the United Nations," Pepito called back.

"That sounds like fun," said Mrs. Pulaski, and she continued to shake her mop.

"I'm going to make a speech there," Pepito told her as he boarded the bus.

The bus pulled away from the curb, leaving Mrs. Pulaski standing on the steps saying "Hm" to herself.

After a short ride Pepito and his father and mother transferred to a crosstown bus. The bus started up and suddenly a taxi drove by, scraping the bus's side. The bus driver stuck his head out the window. The taxi driver stuck his head out his window. The two fussed and argued for a full city block.

Pepito watched them and shook his head. The two drivers were so busy arguing that they

almost drove through a red traffic light.

A policeman's whistle shrilled.

"Where do you think you are going?" yelled the policeman.

The drivers stopped arguing.

"We are going to the United Nations," Pepito shouted to him through the window.

The policeman saw Pepito's smile. "What are you going to do at the United Nations?" he asked.

"I'm going to give a speech," Pepito said.

The policeman scratched his head as the bus started slowly on.

A driver honked his horn. Pepito looked back and saw the policeman walk over and say something to him. Everyone settled down again in the jolting bus—everyone except the driver, who was muttering to himself.

When Pepito and his mother and father climbed off the bus at the United Nations, the driver was still muttering.

A bright ray of sunlight broke through the mist of the East River and spread a glow over the wide city street. Pepito smiled at the driver. The driver stopped muttering and the bus rolled away.

"Well, here we are," said Pepito's father.

They stood for a moment before the United Nations Secretariat Building. It was the same building that Pepito had looked at so many times from his fire escape.

Pepito looked up...and up...and up....The magnificent glass and marble structure towered so high that it seemed to melt into the sky.

Pepito looked down...past the beautiful facade...past the great shining green-tinted windows, down...down...down...until he came to Pepito. He did not feel very big.

"But I will give my speech," he said to himself. "I must!"

"Come, Pepito," said his father. "We shall go to the General Assembly Building."

"Is that where I give my speech?" asked Pepito.

"Pepito—you cannot give a speech here," said his mother worriedly.

"Is the General Assembly Building where other people give their speeches?" Pepito asked his father.

"You might say that," said his father. "That is where the General Assembly Hall is."

"We shall go there," Pepito decided.

They walked down the United Nations Plaza past the long row of flags of all the countries that are members of the United Nations. In the lobby of the General Assembly Building, Pepito and his parents saw a large crowd of people waiting to take tours of the United Nations. As the guide pointed out gifts from different countries, Pepito said to himself, "Friends are worldwide. That is the way it should be."

They saw the mural tapestry "Triumph of Peace" from Belgium, one of the largest and most beautiful tapestries ever woven. There was a ceremonial mantle from Peru over two thousand years old. The Foucault pendulum, a gift from the Netherlands, hung suspended from the ceiling. Its motion back and forth showed the rotation of the earth.

These were only a few of the extraordinary gifts presented to the United Nations by the countries of the world. Each gift had been given in a spirit of brotherhood.

"What do you think of them?" whispered Pepito's father.

"Please," said Pepito, "when can I give my speech?"

It was not that Pepito was uninterested in the things they were seeing on the tour. He just thought it was more important to concentrate on his speech.

"And that, ladies and gentlemen," said the guide, "concludes the tour." They reentered the lobby of the General Assembly Building as the doors of the General Assembly Hall opened. Distinguished men and women of many races and nationalities filed out. Some looked confident, some worried, some were talkative, others silent. Nearly all carried briefcases.

"They are the delegates to the United Nations," Pepito's father told him.

The delegates—to the United Nations? Was the meeting over? Surely not! Pepito hurried to the door just as it was being closed.

He looked inside. Here was the General Assembly Hall where he hoped to give his speech.

No one was there.

Pepito turned silently away.

"They will meet again this afternoon," his mother told him gently. "But Pepito..." She did not finish, for Pepito's face once more was shining like the March sun outside.

Back at the Information Desk the attendant looked searchingly at Pepito. "No," she advised them. "This boy is older than five and younger than twelve. He can be admitted on tours but not to official meetings."

"I have an important speech to make in the General Assembly Hall," Pepito confided to her.

"Little boys are not permitted to make speeches at the United Nations," said the attendant. She turned to answer someone else's question.

"But..."

"Pepito, I have told you that, too," reminded his mother.

Pepito scarcely heard her. Now it was official. The delegates of the United Nations did not want to hear his speech.

"Come, Pepito," said his father kindly. "Let's visit the Coffee Shop and have lunch."

Pepito ate well, for it was not every day that he could dine out, but his mind was still on the problem of giving his speech.

When lunch was over they walked along the Plaza. Pepito's mother, gay in her bright hat and yellow-and-white dress, said, "What shall we do now?"

The next thing they knew, they were standing in the lobby of the General Assembly Building and the guide was asking them, "Are you going to take this tour again?"

"He wants to," Pepito's father said, pointing to Pepito.

The tour started much the same as it had before, but this time Pepito listened carefully to the guide. He learned more about the United Nations because he was not thinking so much about his speech. He knew it perfectly and was sure he would find a way to give it in spite of what the woman at the Information Desk had said.

Pepito listened to the guide speaking of all the gifts to the United Nations. "My speech will be my gift to the United Nations," thought Pepito.

When they returned to the General Assembly Building, Pepito followed his father and mother to a small room beyond the lobby.

"Pepito," his father said, "we shall go into the Meditation Room and think of all the wonderful things we have seen and heard."

At the entrance to the Meditation Room he reminded Pepito that they must be very quiet inside. In a low voice he read from a folder that had been given to him:

This is a room dedicated to peace and those who are giving their lives for peace. It is a room of quiet where only thoughts should speak.

"This is a nice room," whispered Pepito as they entered.

"Shhh!" said his mother.

His father waggled a finger for silence.

It was indeed a room of quiet. Pepito stared

at the huge block in the middle of the room, its surface illuminated by a shaft of light from above. It was a cornerstone or altar for all mankind. Pepito and his mother and father gave themselves to silence; their thoughts were of peace.

Pepito's thoughts soon turned to his speech. He wanted to give it aloud and let others hear his prayer for peace throughout the world.

But Pepito was very tired. He dozed, then fell asleep. And as he slept, he dreamed.

Suddenly, very clearly, he saw a tall, scholarly-looking gentleman with a briefcase under one arm walking toward the General Assembly Hall.

And suddenly Pepito was walking beside him.

The man scarcely glanced at Pepito and Pepito scarcely glanced at him.

"Is that boy with the delegate?" one guide whispered.

Another guide shrugged and said, "He must be."

And the two little feet marched on beside the two big ones. They entered the General Assembly Hall together. The delegate hurried to his seat and Pepito hurried to the front of the room. A guard hurried after him.

"Where are you going, boy?" said the guard, taking Pepito's arm and trying to lead him away.

"Up there," said Pepito, pointing to the place where the Secretary-General stood. "I am going to give a speech."

The guard gripped Pepito's arm more firmly. "You are going this way," he said, turning him back toward the door.

"No, please," said Pepito.

A second guard appeared. "What's happening?" he whispered. "Is this boy related to any of the delegates?"

The first guard had not thought of that. "I don't know," he whispered, "but he can't stay here."

"We don't want to offend anyone," said the other guard.

While they were whispering, one of the delegates of the United Nations rose from his seat and joined them.

"What is the difficulty?" he asked.

They told him.

"Speech?" he said. "A boy can't make a speech here."

"Speech is free," said Pepito.

Another delegate joined the group. He wanted to know what was going on. They told him.

Two other delegates joined them, and soon there was more talking. The Secretary-General banged his gavel. He motioned the guards to bring Pepito to him.

When they reached the Secretary-General, he asked them what was wrong. They told him.

"Please, sir," said Pepito, "I only want to make a speech, like you do. This is a land of free speech, and I am sure there is free speech in the United Nations."

Pepito had arrived at a critical time. There was sharp disagreement among some nations. The Secretary-General had been trying to bring a measure of calm to the heated discussion.

He hesitated a moment, looking at Pepito. Then, being a wise and understanding man, he said, "What is your speech about?"

"Peace," said Pepito. "I want to tell the world how to have peace."

The Secretary-General's grave face relaxed. "It is the fervent prayer of us all," he said. He hesitated again. This was a time of crisis in the Assembly. There was still tension between the disagreeing delegates. Should he let the boy speak? Impossible. Yet…the Secretary-General recalled words of long ago: "A little child shall lead them." Deliberately, he reached for his gavel and rapped for order.

"Distinguished delegates," he said, "we have an unexpected visitor—one who wants to tell us how to have peace."

There was a brief stir. The room quieted.

The Secretary-General's kind face looked out over the large assembly of delegates. He leaned over slowly and said to Pepito, "What is your name?"

Pepito told him.

The Secretary-General straightened up. He

leaned over again. "What did you say?"

Pepito told him again.

The Secretary-General straightened up and pounded for silence. "We have a guest speaker," he advised the United Nations delegates. "His name is Pepito Gustafus Ivanovich Blair."

The delegates of the United Nations, who were accustomed to unusual names, looked surprised. But Pepito knew he had as much right as anyone to be there—perhaps more. In his blood was the blood of ancestors from many nations.

There was another stir, and the Secretary-General rapped his gavel. Pepito had the floor.

Pepito gazed at those seated in front of him—they represented the hope of mankind for a lasting peace. He saw it in the faces of the delegates from every nation. Each of them sat at his place ready to present the views of his government. Together they made up a united world willing to meet and discuss problems in the hope of solving them. Without an opportunity for discussion in these days of high-powered weapons, no hope would remain. It was mankind's only chance for survival.

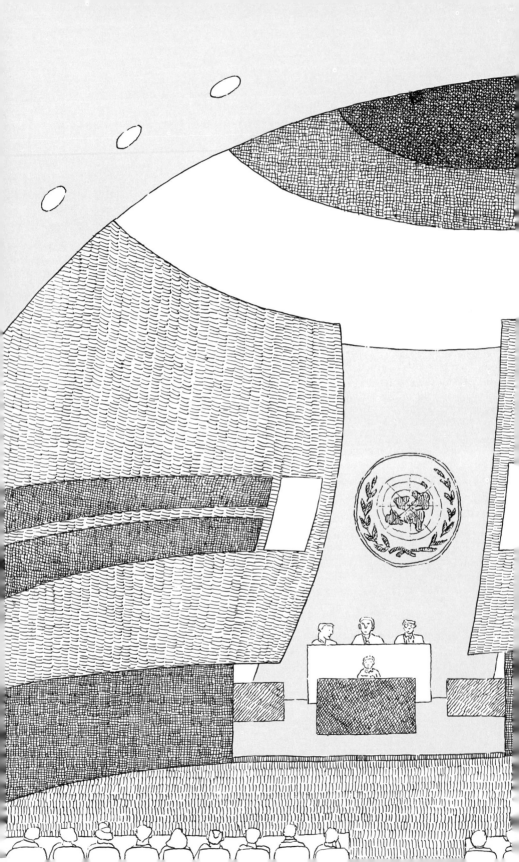

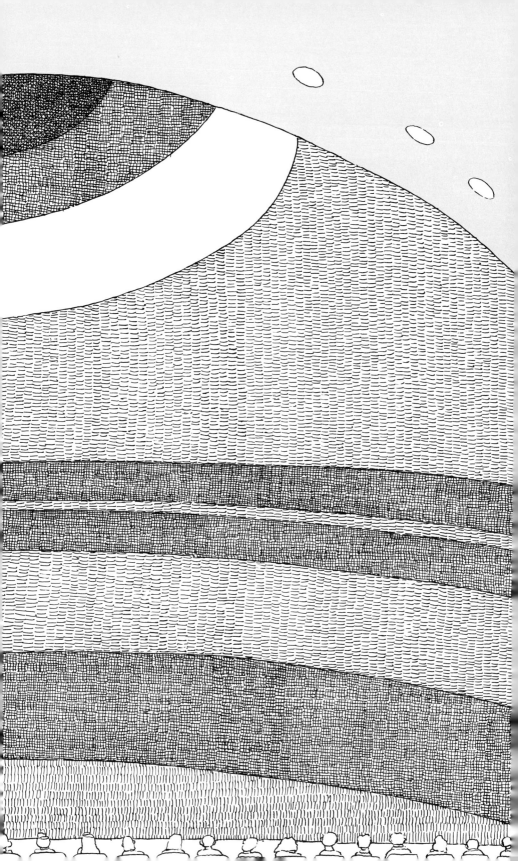

Pepito looked to his right at the people waiting to hear him speak. He looked to the people at his left. He looked at the people in front of him. At his right, among the strangers staring at him, he imagined his friend Mr. Graccioso. At his left he imagined Mr. Roberts. Before him were Mrs. Pulaski, Mrs. Aufheiser, Mrs. Callahan, and Mrs. O'Leary, his other neighbors. Pepito was ready to begin. It was time to concentrate on his speech. He hesitated a moment longer. The Secretary-General tapped his gavel and nodded for Pepito to begin.

Pepito's speech spun around in his head. He could not begin. He did not remember it all. It would not be right to start in the middle or at the end. He must begin at the beginning, but Pepito could not remember how the speech started. Everything vanished in that moment when he stood before the representatives of the nations of the world. He searched the farthest corners of his mind for the speech that would not come. Then he bowed his head.

If ever in his life Pepito had felt miserable, it was now. Here, before the General Assembly of the United Nations, he had made a fool of himself. He could not speak.

He tried again. No word would come. Confused and discouraged, Pepito stood and waited for the world's judgment and mercy. He had done his best, but his best was nothing. He could not even voice the first thought of his grand speech. He could not utter one sound to begin the wonderful flow of ideas that came from his heart. He could not tell them about his discovery that kindness does much good in a disagreeing world, and that to listen at times is also good, for it gives the other person a chance to express his views.

Pepito held out his hands to show his defeat and shook his head. Slowly he looked up and smiled. And as Pepito's smile emerged, it touched those before him with the warmth that came from an understanding heart.

Then, wonder of wonders, Pepito saw something he had never dreamed of—his own smile reflected on the faces of all the delegates from all the countries of the world! Pepito knew that he was among friends though they came from many different nations. A single smile had brought them together. Pepito had not given the speech he had prepared, but his real speech was his smile, and it said more than any words of any language. It said to everyone who saw it: "I am a friend and I offer you friendship." Everyone there seemed to understand, for suddenly they were crowding around Pepito, congratulating him and telling him that his smile was the best speech ever given. Someone tapped him on the shoulder, but the crowd was so great and pressing that Pepito could not turn to see who it was. The tap became stronger and stronger...

Pepito woke up. He was in the room of meditation and his father was shaking his shoulder. It was very quiet.

"You have been asleep," whispered Pepito's father.

"I know," said Pepito. "I did not give my speech. It was only a dream."

"Everybody dreams," Pepito's father said as they left the room and walked through the lobby of the General Assembly Building. "There's nothing wrong with dreaming."

"It is good to smile," said Pepito thoughtfully.

His mother looked puzzled and so did his father, but his mother said wisely, "Then we should smile often."

They went out to the sunlit United Nations Plaza, and Pepito smiled up at his mother and father with a big, broad, sunny smile. They smiled back at him, and so did many people from other countries who were strolling on the wide Plaza past the waving flags of many nations.